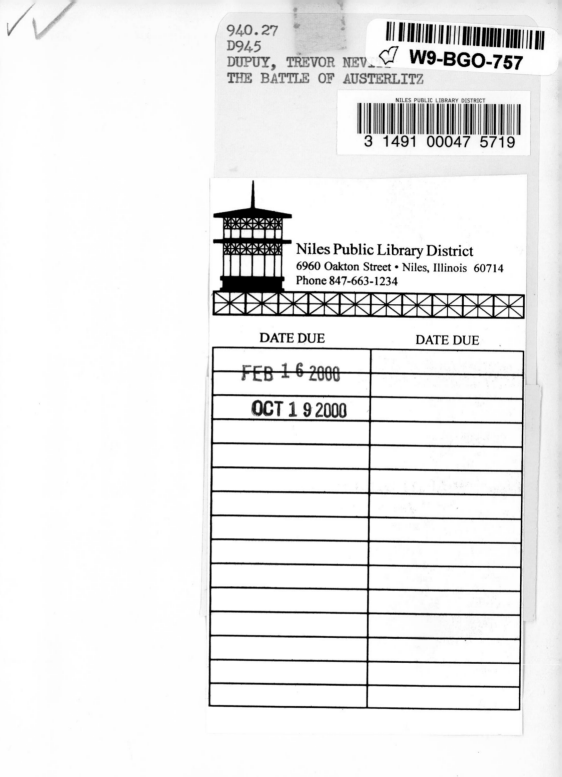

Niles Public Library District

6960 Oakton Street • Niles, Illinois 60714
Phone 847-663-1234

DATE DUE	DATE DUE
FEB 1 6 2000	
OCT 1 9 2000	

The Battle of Austerlitz

Napoleon's Greatest Victory

The Battle

The Macmillan Company, New York
Collier–Macmillan Limited, London

# of Austerlitz

By Trevor N. Dupuy

For Fielding

The Macmillan Company, New York
Collier-Macmillan Canada, Ltd., Toronto, Ontario
Library of Congress catalog card number: 68–24102
Printed in the United States of America

FIRST PRINTING

Maps by Rafael Palacios

PICTURE CREDITS: Culver Pictures, title page, frontispiece, 13, 15, 16, 19, 31
(a,d,e,g), 40–41, 46, 47, 56, 57, 60, 62–63, 73; Historical Pictures Service–Chicago,
6–7, 27, 35, 65, 70, 75; Le Marchant Collection, R.M.A. Sandhurst Central Library, 33; National Maritime Museum, England, 20, 21; Radio Times Hulton
Picture Library, 3, 8–9, 11, 22–23, 26, 31 (c,f), 80–81; Versailles Museum, 24,
52–53; Victoria and Albert Museum, 44. Picture research by Patricia Crum.

Contents

1

To Austerlitz
from Ajaccio

"Before tomorrow night that army
will be in my power!"

The short but impressive figure in
the plain gray, travel-stained greatcoat
spoke vehemently, almost gleefully,
to a group of more colorfully uniformed men gathered in a
semicircle behind him. He swept his arm in an arc to the east,
pointing across a narrow valley to a broad plateau about two
miles away. It was a bright, clear day—and the group of officers
could distinctly see the masses of troops gathering on the opposite heights. Their breath misting in the cold, crisp air, several
of the officers raised spyglasses to their eyes, the better to see
the columns of Russian and Austrian troops streaming through
and around the distant town of Austerlitz to join those already
on the plateau. Now, as the officers stamped their feet to keep
warm, their dynamic leader turned to face them.

He was Napoleon Bonaparte, Emperor of the French. He and

his marshals and senior divisional generals had just finished a chilly lunch near the crest of Zurlon Hill, overlooking his own army stretched out for several miles to the north and south. During the meal he had been explaining his plans. Afterward, Napoleon had led the generals to the top of the hill, to show them that the enemy was acting just as he had expected, assuring the success of his plan. Below, there were puffs of smoke and the sound of firing as French and allied skirmishers clashed.

Now the emperor looked intently at his marshals and generals, a broad smile on his thin lips. "Tomorrow," he repeated, "that army will be mine."

It was December 1, 1805. Here in central Moravia, in the rolling, open country between the cities of Brünn and Austerlitz, the decisive moment was almost at hand. For Napoleon, it was the culmination of three months of careful planning, rapid movement and vigorous action. The next day, as the emperor well knew, would be the first anniversary of his coronation. It would be, he realized, a violent and bloody celebration, but he was certain that it would be a glorious one for him and for his Empire.

In late August and early September, Napoleon had put his divisions in motion from their bases in northern France. Now, after overrunning southern Germany and occupying Vienna, capital of the Hapsburg emperor of Austria and the Holy Roman Empire, he had led a portion of his army into Moravia. Here in the heart of central Europe, sixty miles north of Vienna, his troops were scattered over an area of several miles, with no apparent line of retreat to France except through Vienna.

Napoleon felt certain that his enemies would think that he was dangerously isolated and exposed to attack by their more numerous forces. For more than a week he had done everything in his power to encourage the emperors of Russia and Austria and their generals in that belief. He had withdrawn his outposts from Austerlitz, pretending to avoid battle while he was in fact secretly preparing for it. And now, with the foe gathering near

*Napoleon
Bonaparte*

Austerlitz and on the Heights of Pratzen, he knew that he had completely fooled the enemy. Secretly and quietly he had gathered his scattered troops around him, east of Brünn. He had carefully prepared an alternate line of retreat through Bohemia, just in case the enemy avoided the trap. But now he was confident that his carefully planned retreat line would never be used.

By early afternoon of December 1, as Napoleon and his senior officers ate lunch on Zurlon Hill, he had gathered about 65,000 men, prepared for battle the following day. Only Marshal Louis N. Davout with two divisions of the Third Corps, perhaps 8,000 additional men, had not yet arrived. They had a long way to come—some of them from as far as Vienna. But Napoleon knew Davout; that reliable commander would arrive in time for the battle.

Now, almost gaily, the emperor dismissed his generals, sending them back to their commands to issue their orders and to prepare for the battle. He ordered them to meet him again on the hill by seven thirty the following morning. Napoleon himself mounted his white horse. Accompanied by a small group of his Mameluke Guards, he galloped off to make an inspection of his entire army before the early December dusk.

From the Isle of Corsica

The leader of this army had been born Napoleone Buonaparte on August 15, 1769, in the city of Ajaccio on the rocky island of Corsica off the coast of France in the Mediterranean Sea. He was the second child of Carlo and Letitia di Buonaparte, whose noble ancestors had come to Corsica from Italy more than two hundred years earlier. France had bought Corsica from Genoa (an Italian city-state) the year before Napoleone was born. His birth as a French citizen provided a chance for the exceptionally intelligent lad to get a better education in France than would have been possible in Corsica.

Napoleone entered the military school at Brienne in 1779. There the moody lad, smaller than most of the boys his age, kept much to himself. He was called Napoleon Bonaparte, in the French fashion. His schoolmates teased him, calling him "straw-in-the-nose" because he spoke French with a peculiar accent. But he stood up for himself and they respected him for his spirit.

After five years in the military school, Napoleon was chosen with four other good students in his class to attend the French army's cadet school in Paris. When he graduated a year later, in 1785, young Bonaparte joined an artillery regiment as a second lieutenant. Now barely five feet tall, though still growing, the shy young officer devoted himself to military studies, and particularly to the science of gunnery.

That year Napoleon's father died. Napoleon took on the responsibility of straightening out the family finances. As second son, he was not required to do this, but he had much more drive and ability than his elder brother, Joseph. For the next four years, Napoleon spent much of his time on leave at home in Corsica.

Then, on July 14, 1789, came an event which shook the world. The people of France rose against their king, Louis XVI, and established a republican form of government. It was the beginning of the great upheaval known as the French Revolution. For several years France was in turmoil, as royalists fought bitterly against the republicans in efforts to restore Louis to power.

The neighboring countries of Europe soon began to interfere in this fierce struggle going on inside France. Most of the other European kings wanted to help Louis and his family regain control of France. These rulers felt that the common people had no right to remove a king from his throne; they wanted to destroy the new republican government before ideas of liberty and revolution spread to their own nations. Some of them also thought that the troubles inside France would give them an opportunity to seize French territory, increasing the power of their own countries at the expense of France.

The Siege of Toulon

As a result of these attacks by foreign countries, most of the French people united around their new government and fought vigorously to repel the invaders and suppress the royalists inside France. Young Lieutenant Bonaparte was a strong republican sympathizer, and he responded loyally when his regiment was sent to restore order in the troubled region of southeastern France. By early 1793 he had risen in rank to become a major of artillery.

*July 14, 1789: The fall
of the Bastille*

In the summer and fall of 1793, Major Bonaparte was with a French army trying to recapture the Mediterranean seaport of Toulon. This city had been seized by an invading army composed of English, Spanish, and French royalist soldiers. An English fleet had brought the invaders to Toulon in August. That fleet remained in the harbor to support the occupying troops as they defended Toulon from the French republican army trying to recover the city.

Napoleon at the siege of Toulon

For nearly four months the French army besieged Toulon without success. They were unable to drive the invaders from a strong line of fortifications on the hills ringing the city. Although the attacking army was unsuccessful, young Napoleon Bonaparte did such a fine job in commanding his artillery batteries that he was promoted to colonel.

In December 1793 the young colonel suggested a new plan

of attack. He pointed out that one particular fort, on a high hill overlooking the city, was the key to the defense of Toulon. If the French could capture that, Napoleon was certain that his guns would be able to drive the English fleet out of the harbor. The city would then have to surrender.

Bonaparte's plan was adopted, and he lined up a powerful battery of guns to hammer the walls of the fort. As he was leading one of the columns of French soldiers attacking the stubborn English defenders, Napoleon's horse was shot from under him, so he continued on foot. He was wounded slightly; nevertheless he and his men fought their way into the fort, driving out the English. Bonaparte immediately moved a number of his guns into this fort and directed their fire against the English fleet in the harbor below. Unable to protect themselves against this damaging artillery fire from the captured fort, the English fleet had to withdraw, taking with it the soldiers who had been occupying the city. The French army marched in at once to recapture Toulon.

"A Whiff of Grapeshot"

Because of the part he had played in driving the invaders from Toulon, Napoleon Bonaparte was promoted to brigadier general early in 1794. He was not yet twenty-five years old.

The following year General Bonaparte happened to be in Paris when a serious royalist uprising almost overthrew the Directory—the republican government. The desperate politicians placed him in command of the loyal republican forces in the city.

Napoleon set up artillery pieces in the Paris streets, to protect the Directory from the mobs of royalists. When they attacked, Napoleon opened fire; the deadly grapeshot drove them off in confusion. In a few hours the energetic young general put down

"The whiff of grapeshot": Napoleon fires on royalists in Paris.

the uprising and saved the French Republic. As a reward, General Bonaparte was placed in command of the Army of Italy early in 1796. This army was defending southeastern France from a threatened invasion by the combined armies of Austria and Piedmont, a small, vigorous, independent nation of northwestern Italy, also known as the Kingdom of Sardinia (the duke of Piedmont was also the king of Sardinia).

Shortly before this time, Napoleon met an attractive, partyloving widow six years older than he. Her name was Josephine de Beauharnais. Napoleon fell in love with her and married her on March 9, 1796. He remained devoted to her for many years.

The First Italian Campaign

So far, young Napoleon Bonaparte had been known to few people. He was simply one of many French officers fighting loyally to save their country from foreign invasion, and to prevent the reestablishment of the hated rule of the French kings. Then suddenly, in 1796, this youthful general, commanding a ragged army of French soldiers, invaded northern Italy, where he won a series of amazing victories.

In a few weeks General Bonaparte had conquered all of Piedmont, which he forced to make peace with France. Continuing on, Napoleon's troops defeated four Austrian armies—each larger than his own—and drove them completely out of Italy. Early in 1797 Bonaparte marched northeast through the snowy passes of the Alps to invade Austria and to threaten Vienna itself.

As the French armies approached his capital, Francis II, the Holy Roman Emperor, decided to make peace. His armies were smashed, his generals unable to match the brilliance and energy of this amazing young military genius. On April 18, 1797, Bonaparte dictated the peace terms at Leoben, ninety miles from Vienna. In less than a year he had risen from obscurity to become the most renowned man in Europe.

2

Bonaparte's Rise to Power

After Napoleon Bonaparte's great victories over Piedmont and Austria in 1796 and 1797, England was the only important country remaining at war with the French Republic. But since the English navy controlled both the Atlantic Ocean and the Mediterranean Sea, the French were unable to strike back at England.

Bonaparte knew, however, that England's wealth and power were based on resources in her many colonies beyond the seas. The richest and most tempting of these colonies was India. Unable to reach India by sea, Napoleon reasoned that if he could get to Egypt he could then march overland to India through Syria and Persia, as Alexander the Great had done twenty-one centuries earlier. He believed he could get past the British fleet in the Mediterranean to reach Egypt.

The French government approved Bonaparte's plan. So in

1798 he took an army to Egypt, where he won a number of victories and quickly conquered the country. But he was unsuccessful in getting Turkey to join France against England, as he had hoped.

On August 1, 1798, the English fleet, under young Admiral Horatio Nelson, defeated the French fleet in a great sea battle at Aboukir Bay, near the mouth of the Nile River. Nelson's victory cut off the French army from its overseas link with France. The French soldiers were unfamiliar with the tropical climate and many died of disease. Uprisings among the Egyptian people, combined with Turkish and English attacks by land and sea, finally forced Napoleon to admit defeat. He was able to slip past Nelson's fleet to return to France, but much of his army was lost in Egypt.

Bonaparte Gains Power and Peace

Though Napoleon had failed in his efforts to hold Egypt, the French people were proud of his victories over far larger forces of Egyptian, Turkish, and English troops. When he returned to France, he found himself to be the most popular man in the country. He also discovered that the country was in serious trouble.

While Napoleon was in Egypt, England had gathered new allies in Europe, and France had sustained severe defeats in Italy and Germany. The French government suffered from poor management, and the people were getting very weary of a war that had lasted nearly eight years. In November 1799, hoping to save his country from complete collapse and defeat, Napoleon seized control of the government in a sudden *coup d'état*. He was appointed First Consul and became virtual dictator of France.

Napoleon quickly restored efficient and vigorous government

General Bonaparte with his men in Egypt

in Paris. When the allies spurned his peace offers, he prepared armies to meet invading forces threatening the frontiers of France. The most dangerous of these threats were two powerful Austrian armies, one in Germany, the other in Italy.

Early in 1800 Napoleon sent one army to hold back the Austrians near the Rhine River while he himself led another army in an amazing march across the Alps into northern Italy. A few weeks later he defeated the larger Austrian army in Italy at the Battle of Marengo. Soon afterward the other French army defeated the Austrians in Germany, and again Austria was forced to make peace with Bonaparte.

England was discouraged by the repeated failure of her efforts to overthrow the French Republic. In March 1802 she made peace at the Treaty of Amiens. In August the French people rewarded Napoleon for bringing peace to Europe by electing him First Consul of France for life. This meant that he was practically a king, and was now the most important and successful man in Europe.

First Consul Bonaparte

What sort of man was this who, at the age of thirty, had established himself as the dictatorial ruler of France, and who could force proud emperors and kings to make peace with him on his own terms?

Napoleon Bonaparte was a short man, now slightly more than five feet tall. He was slender, active, restless, with one of the most powerful intellects ever possessed by a human being. All who knew him were captivated by his brilliance and his charm, his friendliness and his generosity.

Many times Bonaparte had personally led his troops into battle with reckless bravery—at Toulon, in Italy, and in Egypt. He had proven to the French soldiers that there was no one in the entire army more courageous than he. Because of this, and because he was always able to outmaneuver and outthink his enemies and thus win victory after victory, no general has been more admired or more adored by his men than was Napoleon Bonaparte.

He was an efficient ruler. He gave France a new and improved school system, and a new set of laws, which is still in use today. He spread the ideals of the French Revolution—liberty and equality for all men—throughout Europe.

That was the good side of this remarkable man. There was also another side.

Napoleon's installation as First Consul

Being much more intelligent than anyone around him, Napoleon had found that it was easy to dominate others and to be successful in anything he attempted. This he had proven, of course, by his amazing victories, and by his rapid rise from obscurity to power. A great reader of history and an admirer of the conquests of such earlier generals as Alexander the Great, Hannibal, and Julius Caesar, Napoleon had dreams of becoming a great conqueror too. He believed that his military genius would enable him to dominate all of Europe. This ambition was destined to spread tragedy throughout his country, and to cause his own downfall.

England Again Seeks Allies

Peace between England and France did not last for much more than a year. Disputes between the two countries broke out almost immediately, and in May 1803 England declared war again.

At first it was a strange war. By this time France had replaced Austria as the most powerful nation on the continent of Europe. She had the best army and the best general in the world. England, on the other hand, was the mistress of the oceans and of a far-flung, worldwide empire held together and protected by the powerful Royal Navy. For two years these mighty antagonists could do little but glare at each other across the narrow English Channel.

England tried to arouse some of the other European nations against France, so that the French would have to fight a land war against several countries at the same time, while the English fleet gave support and assistance off the European seacoast. England offered money to any countries that might be interested in joining such an alliance, to help them raise armies and buy the weapons and equipment necessary to make war.

But although many nations of the continent still hated the

The Battle of Marengo: June 14, 1800

French and feared Napoleon, the English did not at first have much success in their efforts to obtain allies. The other European nations doubted that they could stop the invincible French armies and their great general, even with British support. The smaller countries would not join England unless the larger nations did so too. But Russia, Austria, and Prussia did not trust each other—or England either—enough to form an alliance, and none was strong enough to fight France alone.

Russia, under Czar Alexander I, had her own border disputes with Turkey and Persia. Furthermore, the young Russian emperor saw himself as the peacemaker of Europe. As a result, instead of joining with England in her war against France, Alexander tried to bring France and England together to make peace.

Austria was eager to avenge the many defeats which Napoleon and other French generals had inflicted upon her during the French revolutionary wars. She wished to win back the territory she had lost. Emperor Francis II was also anxious to overthrow

Flat-bottomed boats for the French Navy's planned invasion of England

the French government because he was fearful that ideas of liberty and revolution, spreading from France, might lead to unrest and revolt in his own lands. But the memory of the defeats his empire had suffered at the hands of Napoleon was still fresh. Francis and his advisers let England know that they would be happy to join in the alliance against France if they saw any chance of success—but they saw none at that time.

The new king of Prussia, Frederick William III, had no particular reason to oppose France or Napoleon. Furthermore, his small but powerful country had longstanding rivalries with Russia, Austria, and England. So Prussia decided not to join the proposed alliance.

Bonaparte, meanwhile, established a strong army on the

northern French seacoast at Boulogne, overlooking the Strait of
Dover. This was the narrowest part of the English Channel. Only
twenty-two miles of water separated England from France. At
the same time he made strenuous efforts to rebuild the French
navy so that it could challenge England's control of the sea. He
believed that if he could concentrate enough ships in the English
Channel to gain control of that narrow body of water, even for
a few days, he could cross with his army and quickly conquer
England. By early 1804 all the preparations had been completed.
Napoleon had gathered 190,000 men, as well as two thousand
flat-bottomed barges to carry the troops across the Channel.
The French Navy had only to defeat, or to trick, the English
fleet.

Emperor Napoleon and the Third Coalition

Then, in May of 1804, an event occurred which was to have immediate and widespread repercussions. Napoleon decided that he should become Emperor of France. An election was held, and the French people overwhelmingly voted their approval. On December 2, 1804, the Pope came to Paris from Rome to preside over Napoleon's coronation. At the climax of the ceremony, Napoleon took the crown from the hands of the astonished Pope, and crowned himself Napoleon I, Emperor of the French. Then he crowned Josephine Empress.

This event helped to change matters for the Russian Czar. He was annoyed by Napoleon's presumption in making himself

The coronation of Napoleon, by David

emperor, since Napoleon was not of royal blood. He also felt that Napoleon had not helped his attempts to make peace between France and England. So, early in 1805, the Russians began to show more interest in joining Britain against France.

For several months secret negotiations went on between England and Russia. When the Austrian emperor learned that Russia was willing to fight France, he also decided to join the alliance. He was sure that Napoleon was so intent upon an invasion of England that he would be unable to prevent a combined Austro-Russian army from driving the French from their footholds in Germany and northern Italy. So the Austrians, Russians, and English, joined by Sweden and Naples, established the alliance known as the Third Coalition. They began to plan a joint invasion of France. Prussia remained neutral.

3

La Grande Armée on the March

Meanwhile, Napoleon was poised to
strike at England. All that was necessary was to seize control of the
English Channel long enough for his
army to cross to Britain. He ordered
Admiral Pierre de Villeneuve, commanding the French fleet, to
clear the British from the Channel "for only six hours," which
the emperor estimated was all he needed to make the crossing.
But Napoleon was no sailor, nor had he the same mastery of
movement at sea that he had on land. Furthermore, the English
Navy refused to cooperate. As summer wore on, Villeneuve
was unable to create the conditions necessary for the invasion.

Napoleon's spies had been keeping him informed of the secret
negotiations that were leading to the establishment of the Third
Coalition. By midsummer he had learned that Austria and Russia
had begun to mobilize their armies in preparation for a move
against France.

To Napoleon, the master plan of his adversaries was transto interfere with the Austrian advance, but if they did, he felt sure that they could not reach Bavaria until the middle of November. By that time, he knew that the two Russian armies under Kutuzov and Buxhöwden would have joined him, giving the allies overwhelming strength in central Germany. General Mack did not expect any serious French resistance until he and the Russians reached the Rhine.

But when General Mack's Austrian army marched into Bavaria, early in September, the Elector of Bavaria was enraged. He made an alliance with Napoleon. The little Bavarian army of 20,000 men was ready to join the French Grand Army. And Napoleon's army—all unknown to General Mack—was already rushing at full speed from the Strait of Dover toward the Rhine River.

The Grand Army Crosses the Rhine

On September 2, as soon as the last unit of his Grand Army had left Boulogne, Napoleon returned to Paris. This was part of his scheme to keep the allies from learning about his plans to move his army to central Germany. At the same time he ordered the utmost secrecy to prevent anyone from learning anything about the advance of his soldiers.

Under cover of this secrecy the French army marched steadily to the southeast. Day after day the French soldiers marched fifteen to twenty-five miles, without rest and without break. Speed and secrecy accomplished what Napoleon wanted. On September 26, at the very time that the entire French army was crossing the Rhine and entering Germany, the Austrians and the other allies thought that Napoleon was still in Paris, and that the French soldiers were still in their camps at Boulogne. As a matter of fact, Napoleon joined his army that day on the banks of the Rhine River.

General Mack, meanwhile, had moved his army to Ulm, in Bavaria, and taken up a position covering the lines of the Iller and Danube rivers. There he awaited the arrival of the Russians. Mack had about 50,000 men in and around Ulm.

Suddenly Mack learned that the French were advancing against him. The French cavalry, under Marshal Murat, had crossed the Rhine from Alsace and was plunging ahead toward the mountainous Black Forest. Word of this movement quickly reached Mack, who disposed his men to meet an expected French move through the Black Forest passes. What he did not know was that Murat had left only a handful of troops in the western fringes of the Black Forest, and had shifted all of his 22,000-man cavalry corps rapidly to the north, to form an impenetrable screen in front of the seven French infantry corps now rushing into central Germany.

On the left flank of the Grand Army was the First Corps, 15,000 strong, commanded by Marshal Jean Baptiste Bernadotte, a swaggering soldier with a shock of black hair and a big, sharply pointed nose. Bernadotte was descending from Hanover through Ansbach into Bavaria. Marshal Auguste Marmont, who had become friendly with Napoleon during the siege of Toulon in 1793, was marching from Holland with the Second Corps of 20,000 men. He had joined Bernadotte at Würzburg, and then had continued on, to the right of, and abreast of, the First Corps.

The coldly efficient Marshal Louis Nicolas Davout had marched from the region near Boulogne with the 25,000 troops of the Third Corps, and was now marching just to the right—or west—of Marmont. Davout was a first-rate soldier from an aristocratic family of whom it was said, "Whenever a Davout is born, it is a sword that has come out of its scabbard." Further to the southwest was Marshal Nicolas Soult's Fourth Corps, 37,000 strong. A short bowlegged man, Soult was an old soldier who had risen from the ranks to become one of Napoleon's most trusted subordinates.

RIGHT: *Marshals of the Grand Army: (a) Bernadotte (b) Marmont (c) Davout (d) Ney (e) Lannes (f) Soult (g) Augereau*

(a)

(b)

(c)

(d)

(e)

(f)

(g)

Just to the south and west came the 16,000 troops of Marshal
Jean Lannes's Fifth Corps. This brave, energetic and thoroughly
elegant soldier was called "the Roland of the army." On the
right of the army marched the Sixth Corps, under Marshal
Michel Ney, an excellent rider and swordsman whose principal
hope and desire was to gain military fame. Following behind
were the 12,000 men of Marshal Charles Pierre Augereau's
Seventh Corps, which had been stationed in Brittany and thus
had the greatest distance to march.

Each corps marched in several parallel columns along roads
selected earlier by Napoleon. In each of these columns the order
of march was two smaller columns on either side of the road,
leaving the center free for messengers and vehicles. Generals
led the way on horseback.

A Shock for General Mack

General Mack, encamped near Ulm, remained happily unaware
of the nearness of the Grand Army. He had his eye still trained
on the Black Forest, where his attention had been attracted by
Murat's feint. He was also alert for a possible advance by Marshal
Massena from Italy through Switzerland. He was sure that he
would be ready for any French move.

Furthermore, Mack expected the Russians to join him by
mid-October. This, he was certain, would be long before the
French could possibly arrive near Ulm. Suddenly, during the
first days of October, Mack received reports that French cavalry
had reached the Danube River near Donauwörth. To Mack's
dismay, French troops were actually closer to Vienna than was
his own army!

Pressing forward with undiminished speed despite cold, damp,
miserable weather, troops of the Third, Fourth, and Fifth French
Corps began to cross the Danube between the towns of Donauwörth and Ingolstadt on October 7, turning southwest behind
Murat's cavalry. Two days later the First and Second Corps

A 19th century watercolor of General Mack after the Battle of Ulm

crossed near Ingolstadt and turned southeast. This put Napoleon's entire army on the road between Ulm and Vienna.

General Mack now realized that his line of retreat to Austria had been cut off by an army at least three times the size of his own. Frantically, he made a desperate effort to escape the trap by marching to the north, but on October 13 his troops were repulsed at Elchingen by troops of Ney's Sixth Corps. Now realizing that he was completely trapped and that there was no way of escape, Mack surrendered with most of his army on October 17. Only a few Austrian troops under Archduke Ferdinand were able to slip out and get back to Austria.

The surrender of an entire Austrian army at Ulm gave Napoleon an amazing and tremendous victory with very little fighting. Although the total forces of the allies outnumbered his own by almost two to one, Napoleon had succeeded in cutting off and capturing an important part of the enemy's forces. He had done this by keeping his own army closely massed and marching with great rapidity. The French soldiers began to grumble, only half jokingly, "The emperor has found a new method to make war; he uses only our legs and not our bayonets."

On to Vienna

Napoleon gave his men no rest. One Austrian army might have been wiped out but other Austrian and Russian armies were still in the field. Although the weather was miserably damp and cold and the roads were deep in mud from constant rains, he ordered his troops to march toward Austria as rapidly as they could. By this time General Kutuzov, with part of his Russian army, had joined the remaining Austrian troops in the Danube Valley west of Vienna. This combined force, about 60,000 strong, now blocked Napoleon's path to the Austrian capital.

By early November Napoleon's troops had crossed the Inn River and begun to invade Austria. The incessant rains had stopped. The days were now dry and cold but Napoleon's men were warmly dressed. Most of the French army moved along the south bank of the Danube, while a small portion scouted to its north.

Napoleon knew that the Austrian armies in Italy and the Tyrol, totaling 150,000 men, would be able to strike his right flank or to cut his line of communications to France if they could get across the Alps. To prevent this, and to keep them from interfering with his advance toward Vienna, Napoleon sent three corps (Augereau's Seventh, Ney's Sixth, and Marmont's Second) to seize all the mountain passes from Italy and the Tyrol into Germany. As a result, Archduke Charles's Austrian army in Italy could reach Vienna only by a long, roundabout march south of the Alps and through Hungary. To prevent this from occurring quickly, Napoleon ordered Marshal André Massena, in command of the French troops in Italy, to keep the Austrians occupied there. Massena did this very well.

Napoleon leading his soldiers on to Vienna

The main body of Napoleon's rapidly advancing army now began to meet resistance from Kutuzov's Russian and Austrian soldiers. But the concentrated French army greatly outnumbered Kutuzov, so the Russians drew back along the Danube River in the direction of Vienna. Kutuzov hoped to slow down Napoleon's advance so that Buxhöwden's Russian army and Archduke Charles's Austrian army could reach Vienna before the French.

Despite Napoleon's successes, Russian Czar Alexander still hoped to strike the French a crippling blow. For some time now he had been making overtures to Frederick William III of Prussia. That monarch consented at last to a meeting with the Russian emperor somewhere near the frontier. Frederick specified that it would have to remain secret so he could keep up his public pose of neutrality. Alexander, pretending that he had misunderstood, appeared at Berlin, the Prussian capital. There his visit had to be made public, much to the annoyance of Frederick William. Alexander did manage, however, to arrange a secret treaty which assured the allies of Prussian support against the French. The iron hand of the Third Coalition was tightening about the French and their emperor.

At that moment Napoleon received shattering news. The French fleet had fought a battle with the British under Lord Nelson off Cape Trafalgar and had suffered an overwhelming defeat. Britain now had an even more powerful stranglehold on the seas. Even though Napoleon was intent on his immediate battle plans, he had a scathing note sent to Admiral Villeneuve who, a few months later, committed suicide.

On November 11, Kutuzov attacked a small section of the French army marching north of the Danube under Marshal Edouard Mortier. By concentrating nearly 30,000 Russians against 12,000 French at Durrenstein, Kutuzov was able to inflict a sharp defeat on Mortier, and he completely stopped this part of the French advance.

But while the Russians were winning this minor battle north

and Danube rivers. There he awaited the arrival of the Russians. Mack had about 50,000 men in and around Ulm.

Suddenly Mack learned that the French were advancing against him. The French cavalry, under Marshal Murat, had crossed the Rhine from Alsace and was plunging ahead toward the mountainous Black Forest. Word of this movement quickly reached Mack, who disposed his men to meet an expected French move through the Black Forest passes. What he did not know was that Murat had left only a handful of troops in the western fringes of the Black Forest, and had shifted all of his 22,000-man cavalry corps rapidly to the north, to form an impenetrable screen in front of the seven French infantry corps now rushing into central Germany.

On the left flank of the Grand Army was the First Corps, 15,000 strong, commanded by Marshal Jean Baptiste Bernadotte, a swaggering soldier with a shock of black hair and a big, sharply pointed nose. Bernadotte was descending from Hanover through Ansbach into Bavaria. Marshal Auguste Marmont, who had become friendly with Napoleon during the siege of Toulon in 1793, was marching from Holland with the Second Corps of 20,000 men. He had joined Bernadotte at Würzburg, and then had continued on, to the right of, and abreast of, the First Corps.

The coldly efficient Marshal Louis Nicolas Davout had marched from the region near Boulogne with the 25,000 troops of the Third Corps, and was now marching just to the right—or west—of Marmont. Davout was a first-rate soldier from an aristocratic family of whom it was said, "Whenever a Davout is born, it is a sword that has come out of its scabbard." Further to the southwest was Marshal Nicolas Soult's Fourth Corps, 37,000 strong. A short bowlegged man, Soult was an old soldier who had risen from the ranks to become one of Napoleon's most trusted subordinates.

RIGHT: *Marshals of the Grand Army: (a) Bernadotte (b) Marmont (c) Davout (d) Ney (e) Lannes (f) Soult (g) Augereau*

to interfere with the Austrian advance, but if they did, he felt sure that they could not reach Bavaria until the middle of November. By that time, he knew that the two Russian armies under Kutuzov and Buxhöwden would have joined him, giving the allies overwhelming strength in central Germany. General Mack did not expect any serious French resistance until he and the Russians reached the Rhine.

But when General Mack's Austrian army marched into Bavaria, early in September, the Elector of Bavaria was enraged. He made an alliance with Napoleon. The little Bavarian army of 20,000 men was ready to join the French Grand Army. And Napoleon's army—all unknown to General Mack—was already rushing at full speed from the Strait of Dover toward the Rhine River.

The Grand Army Crosses the Rhine

On September 2, as soon as the last unit of his Grand Army had left Boulogne, Napoleon returned to Paris. This was part of his scheme to keep the allies from learning about his plans to move his army to central Germany. At the same time he ordered the utmost secrecy to prevent anyone from learning anything about the advance of his soldiers.

Under cover of this secrecy the French army marched steadily to the southeast. Day after day the French soldiers marched fifteen to twenty-five miles, without rest and without break. Speed and secrecy accomplished what Napoleon wanted. On September 26, at the very time that the entire French army was crossing the Rhine and entering Germany, the Austrians and the other allies thought that Napoleon was still in Paris, and that the French soldiers were still in their camps at Boulogne. As a matter of fact, Napoleon joined his army that day on the banks of the Rhine River.

General Mack, meanwhile, had moved his army to Ulm, in Bavaria, and taken up a position covering the lines of the Iller

Marshal Joachim Murat

Napoleon had at his disposal a new kind of army, one conditioned by the Revolution and his own brand of military genius, one which represented a sharp break with tradition. It was called *La Grande Armée*, or the Grand Army. Hitherto, warfare, known as "the sport of kings," had usually been conducted by small bodies of highly trained professionals—either hired mercenaries or recruits from the impoverished peasantry.

The Grand Army was a citizens' army, drawn from all classes with each soldier trained and equipped to do what he could do best. Although the army was accompanied by a well-organized, completely equipped supply train, Napoleon followed the custom established by the Revolutionary armies of having his troops "live off the country." Every day foraging parties gathered food from the area where the units were camped. This saved much time and trouble. It also meant that the supply wagons would be full when they were needed.

On August 28, 1805, the Grand Army marched eastward from its camps in and around Boulogne and in northern Germany. With seven corps of infantry and one cavalry corps, the army totaled about 195,000 men. In addition, Napoleon had another army of about 50,000 men in northern Italy, under the command of Marshal André Massena.

Allied Preparations

To oppose the French the Coalition was mobilizing armies totaling about half a million men, twice the strength of Napoleon's
field armies. Austria had over 260,000 soldiers ready to fight in
Germany and Italy, and Russia was prepared to send 170,000
more. Sweden, Naples, and England all promised contingents.
The Russians, Austrians, and English were sure that they would
have little trouble driving the French out of Italy and Germany.
Then they planned to invade France.

Early in September, Austria and Russia each prepared two
principal armies for action; they planned to have still larger
forces later. The allies expected that Italy would be the principal
theater of the coming conflict, as it had been in 1796, 1799, and
1800. For this reason, the largest Austrian army, about 120,000
men, was stationed in Italy under the Archduke Charles, Austria's best general. The Archduke Ferdinand commanded a
second Austrian army of about half that size, in western Austria.

But Ferdinand was only a figurehead commander; the real
leader of this Austrian army was his Chief of Staff, elderly, ex-
perienced General Karl Mack von Lieberich. General Mack,
as he was commonly called, was responsible for keeping the
French from invading Germany. Two Russian armies were
already marching to join Mack near the Rhine River. Under
the command of General Mikhail Kutuzov, one of these (some
60,000 men) had already arrived in northeastern Austria. The
other, commanded by General Friederich von Buxhöwden, was
marching through Poland, and its 50,000 soldiers would reach
Austria a few weeks later. Then the combined armies expected
to cross the Rhine into France.

On September 2, General Mack began his advance toward
the Rhine. In order to reach that river, he had to march through
Bavaria. Mack did not really expect that the French would try

of position. The Austrian regiments have been dispersed into Italy, in the Tyrol, to camp at Wels and in Bohemia. Have my various ministers written to, in Vienna, Munich, Salzburg, Dresden, Ratisbon, and Berne, and let subscriptions be taken out for the German newspapers of these towns for the person entrusted with the job. All the German papers resound with nothing but the names and movements of Austrian regiments. This matter is very important.

"I should like you to let me have on Monday the box that I am to keep in which the distribution of regiments will be accurately made."

Meanwhile, Marshal Joachim Murat, accompanied by General Henri J. Bertrand, took a trip through western Germany. The two soldiers were disguised as civilians on a business trip. They carefully observed all features of the countryside, particularly the condition of roads and bridges. They also noted all evidence of planned Austrian military movements.

On August 26 everything was ready. Orders were issued for the army to start its movement two days later.

The Emperor addresses his troops at the French camp in Boulogne.

parent. The allies, under England's leadership, hoped that while Napoleon's attention was focused on the English Channel, Russia and Austria could launch a destructive surprise attack against his rear. He now gave up his plan to invade England. Instead he would secretly hurl his vast army against the unsuspecting Russians and Austrians while they were still completing their mobilization. There would indeed be a surprise attack—but it was the intended surprisers who would be surprised.

French Preparations

Before the troops actually began to move, Napoleon rapidly but thoroughly completed his plans for their advance. Using excellent maps prepared by a cartographer named Bacier d'Albe, he made himself intimately familiar with the terrain over which both his own soldiers and those of the enemy were to pass. The locations of every French and allied division were shown by red and black pins stuck in large-scale maps of the countries of central Europe displayed in Napoleon's headquarters. For Napoleon's convenience every mountain range was shown, as was every river to be crossed, and every hamlet which might provide billeting. Assisted by his principal *aide de camp*, General A. Jean Savary, Napoleon calculated the ground to be covered in each day's march and decided the position in which every corps would find itself at every nightfall.

Some idea of the thoroughness with which Napoleon made his preparations may be gained from a letter which he wrote to his Chief of Staff, Marshal Louis Alexandre Berthier, in that summer of 1805.

> "Follow the movements of the Austrian regiments and sort them into the compartments of a box you were to have made for that purpose.
> "The name and number of each regiment should be written on a card, and the compartment changed according to changes

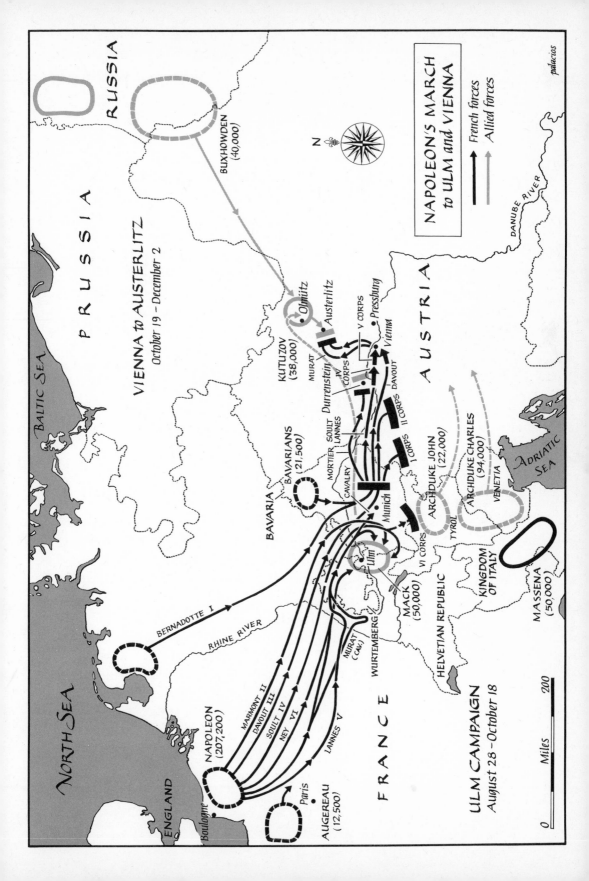

NORTH SEA

ENGLAND

Boulogne

Paris

FRANCE

RHINE RIVER

BERNADOTTE I

MARMONT II
DAVOUT III
SOULT IV
NEY VI
LANNES V

NAPOLEON (207,200)

AUGEREAU (12,500)

BALTIC SEA

PRUSSIA

RUSSIA

BUXHOWDEN (40,000)

N

VIENNA to AUSTERLITZ
October 19 – December 2

Olmütz
Austerlitz

KUTUZOV (38,000)

MURAT
Dürrenstein

V CORPS · Pressburg
IV CORPS · Vienna

MORTIER
SOULT
LANNES

CAVALRY

II CORPS DAVOUT

I CORPS

BAVARIANS (21,500)

BAVARIA

Munich

Ulm

MACK (50,000)

MURAT (CAV.)

WÜRTEMBERG

HELVETIAN REPUBLIC

VI CORPS

ARCHDUKE JOHN (22,000)

TYROL

ARCHDUKE CHARLES (94,000)

VENETIA

KINGDOM OF ITALY

MASSENA (50,000)

AUSTRIA

ADRIATIC SEA

DANUBE RIVER

NAPOLEON'S MARCH
to ULM and VIENNA

→ French forces
→ Allied forces

palacios

ULM CAMPAIGN
August 28 – October 18

0   Miles   200

of the Danube, the rest of the French army continued to rush eastward toward Vienna along the south bank of the river. The Russians and the Austrians had been so intent upon stopping the French advance at Durrenstein that they did not leave enough troops in the Austrian capital to prevent the French from marching into the city.

Only a single bridge spanned the Danube at Vienna. This was protected by Austrian troops under Prince John of Liechtenstein. They had set great kegs of gunpowder under the bridge arches, to destroy the bridge so that the French could not use it. As the French columns marched through Vienna and gathered in great numbers on the river bank near the southern edge of the bridge, the Austrians prepared to light the fuses on the kegs.

At that moment, Marshals Murat and Lannes rode out in front of their troops, calling out that there was an armistice. They dismounted and walked out on the bridge to talk to the Austrian colonel in command of the defending troops. Many of these Austrian soldiers were carrying lighted matches, ready to set off the explosive charges.

The confused Austrian officer had heard nothing about an armistice, but he felt he could not ignore the friendly greeting of the two distinguished French leaders. While he was talking to Murat and Lannes, some of the French soldiers, pretending to be looking around idly, wandered toward the bridge. Suddenly they rushed onto the span, while Murat and Lannes seized the Austrian colonel. A few of the defending soldiers opened fire, and some of them tried to explode the powder kegs. But the French were too quick for them.

In a moment the bridge had been seized, all of the matches had been thrown into the river, and a line of French skirmishers was driving the surprised Austrians away from the northern edge of the bridge. Immediately the French columns began to march again, crossing the bridge in great numbers, and driving the remaining allied troops completely away from Vienna.

Advance into Moravia

Napoleon now saw his chance to cut off Kutuzov's retreating Russian and Austrian army, still near Durrenstein. The second Russian army under Buxhöwden had reached Bohemia. Napoleon hoped to come between these two allied armies before they joined forces. He ordered Murat to advance northward as rapidly as possible, with his cavalry and Lannes's Fifth Corps, so as to cut off Kutuzov's line of retreat to the northeast. Then he himself hastened through Vienna with several more divisions, following Murat.

But Kutuzov, using the same kind of trickery that had enabled the French to seize the Vienna bridge, now fooled Murat into thinking that an armistice was being negotiated between the French and Russian emperors. While Murat stopped near Hollabrunn to permit these pretended negotiations to continue, Kutuzov marched his army rapidly to the north and placed all of his troops ahead of the French cavalry leader.

Leaving the troops under Davout and Mortier to hold Vienna, Napoleon rushed to the front and furiously ordered Murat to resume the advance. But it was too late. Although the French drove back the Russian rear guard in an engagement at Hollabrunn on November 15, Kutuzov was able to keep in front of the pursuers. On November 19 the retreating Russians and Austrians joined the other Russian army near Olmütz, in Bohemia. Kutuzov and Buxhöwden had met at last.

The combined allied armies now came under the command of the Russian Emperor Alexander, although Kutuzov (Alexander's Chief of Staff) really made the plans and issued the orders. Francis, the emperor of Austria, also joined the allied army at Olmütz. About three fourths of this army was Russian and about one fourth was Austrian. Its total strength was 89,000 men.

The French army's
triumphal entry
into Vienna

4

The Emperors Set Their Traps

With the imperial armies of Russia and Austria massed near Olmütz, Napoleon moved his headquarters to Brünn. Knowing that he would soon need his exhausted troops to perform their best in the approaching clash, the French emperor gave them a chance to recover from their long, hard marches. They must be well rested.

While alert French guards and outposts were vigilant to prevent surprise, most of the troops relaxed around roaring campfires, joking and telling stories. But at the same time they busied themselves with cleaning their equipment and repairing torn clothing. Their once brilliant blue and white uniforms, bright with facings of red and other colors, were now worn, torn and shabby. But all soldiers had been kept well supplied with strong, sturdy shoes, and the officers made sure that each man had his weapons—musket, bayonet, and cavalry saber—bright, clean,

and well oiled. And now, with boots well shined, crossbelts
pipe-clayed white again, brass buttons glistening in the thin
autumn sun, the tough French veterans once more looked like
parade-ground soldiers as well as fighters.

Napoleon had started the campaign with about 220,000 men,
including the forces of his German allies. But during the advance
he had had to detach many units. He had left some of his forces
behind to hold the regions conquered in his invasion of Austria.
Three corps had gone to block the passes through the Alps.
Even the remaining force—now reduced to about 100,000 men—
was divided between Vienna and Brünn. Half of these, in the
main army, were in the vicinity of Brünn, in Moravia, spread
out to gather food from the countryside. Another 21,000 were
in Vienna itself, with detachments thrown out as far to the east
as Pressburg (now called Bratislava). About 24,000 occupied
the region north of the Danube River, between Vienna and
Moravia.

Napoleon knew that the Austrians and Russians were anxious
to recapture Vienna. For that reason, he encouraged them to
think that they could easily slip through between his main army
at Brünn and his units in Vienna. He set his men to work digging
trenches as if he were fearful of an attack. He also pulled back
Murat's most advanced cavalry outposts.

Napoleon had guessed what was going on in the minds of the
Austrian and Russian emperors and generals. On November 24,
since he was apparently on the defensive at Brünn, the allies
decided to march to cut the French line of communications to
Vienna. They knew their army was much bigger than that
which Napoleon had in and around Brünn. Also they hoped that
the Archduke Charles would be able to march to meet them at
Vienna and help them overwhelm the French completely. They
did not know that south of the Alps the archduke was being
engaged by Massena and kept too busy to march to Austria.

In order to get as much information as possible about the

allied army and its intentions, on November 26 Napoleon sent his trusted aide, General Jean Savary, with a message to Emperor Alexander, suggesting possible peace negotiations. For the next two days Savary carried several messages back and forth between the French and Russian emperors. Napoleon made certain that this exchange did not lead to any serious peace negotiations— but he learned much about the allied army from the observant Savary.

On November 28, Savary reported to Napoleon that the confident allied army had already begun to march southwest from Olmütz. The French emperor immediately sent orders for Marshal Davout to come up from Pressburg with part of his corps to join the main army. Napoleon also gathered together around Austerlitz all of his other troops in Bohemia, and ordered some of his men up from Vienna. Thus by November 30 he had about 65,000 men assembled in the region between Brünn and Austerlitz, and Davout with 8,000 more was marching to join him.

Meanwhile, on November 29, Savary had returned from his last trip to the allied camp accompanied by Prince Dolgoroulki, one of the Russian emperor's aides. Alexander had guessed Napoleon's real reason for sending Savary as a messenger, and he decided to try to get similar information about the French. But Napoleon had given strict instructions that no allied officers were to come past the French outposts near Austerlitz. When he learned that Dolgoroulki was waiting at the outpost, Napoleon went personally to the outpost to talk to the Russian officer instead of letting him come to the French headquarters. At the same time he ordered some of his men to put on a show for Dolgoroulki's benefit.

Nothing came of the discussion, but Dolgoroulki was able to see small parties of Napoleon's soldiers feverishly digging entrenchments, while French officers nearby were worriedly

Napoleon I, Emperor of France

*Czar Alexander I
of Russia*

whispering to each other, pointing in the direction of the allied army, then shaking their heads in discouragement. Napoleon's guile accomplished the intended result. The allied generals were overjoyed to receive Dolgoroulki's report about the poor condition of the French army. Their only worry was that Napoleon might be so afraid that he would retreat before they had a chance to catch up with him to fight a battle.

When they approached Austerlitz on November 30, therefore, the allies were very pleased to discover that Napoleon and his army were still nearby. Now they thought they could trap the French emperor by moving around his right flank, to cut his line of communications and prevent more reinforcements from coming up from Vienna.

Napoleon realized that the Russian and Austrian emperors thought they had him trapped. But this did not bother him. He was laying a trap of his own. He was not concerned about his line of communications back through Vienna. Even if he should

*Emperor Francis II
of Austria*

be defeated—and he did not expect this—he knew he could retreat
westward through Bohemia and Germany.

He planned to make it easy for the allies to get around his
right flank. Although his army was located on high ground just
west of Austerlitz, on the plateau of Pratzen, he decided to pull
back from this good defensive ground, in order to make it even
easier for the allies to attack him. As he wrote later, he knew he
could win "an ordinary battle" by staying on the high ground—
but he wanted more than an ordinary victory.

The Battlefield

The battlefield that Napoleon had selected was the open, but
rather hilly, countryside in the region between the city of Brünn
and the town of Austerlitz, about 12 miles to the east. Almost
midway the little Goldbach Brook flows south in a deep, narrow

valley that is dominated on the east by the Heights of Pratzen. The brook rises further north in several small rivulets among higher, rocky hills, which were heavily wooded, and not suitable for large-scale military operations. Just south of these wooded hills, the two principal branches of the brook were crossed by the main road, which ran almost directly west into Brünn from Olmütz. The two branches of the brook join about two miles further south, near the town of Kobelnitz, which lies below the northwestern portion of the Pratzen plateau. Continuing southward past Sokolnitz Castle, perched on a bluff just west of the stream, and then past the towns of Sokolnitz and Tellnitz, the swift-flowing Goldbach Brook formed a serious obstacle to troop movements, but it was shallow enough to be forded at any point.

The southern limit of the battlefield was formed by two large ponds situated among more rugged hills. Extremely cold weather during the last few days of November had covered these ponds with a crust of ice which grew thicker every day. Flowing into these ponds from the northeast was the marshy Littawa River, skirting the eastern and southern faces of the Pratzen plateau. This stream, too, was easily crossed by soldiers on foot and on horse, since the swamps had been frozen solid.

Napoleon had decided that he would encourage the allied emperors to try to carry out their apparent plan of moving around his right flank to cut off his line of communications with Vienna. So, as he pulled his army back behind the Goldbach Brook, he concentrated most of his troops in the northern part of the battlefield near the Brünn-Olmütz road. He posted only one weak division along the lower portions of the brook, around the little villages of Sokolnitz and Tellnitz, down toward the frozen ponds of Satschan and Menitz. He wanted to make sure that when the allies reached the Heights of Pratzen, overlooking the Goldbach Valley, they would be able to see how few French soldiers were posted in that area. He felt certain that this would lead the Russians and Austrians to send a large part of their army to try to overwhelm this weak right flank, while the rest of their army attacked down the road toward Brünn. In this way they would expect to crush the French army between these two portions of their army.

But Napoleon planned to have Marshal Davout's corps hidden in the hills behind Sokolnitz and Tellnitz to slow down the expected attack on his right flank. Then, with the two wings of the allied army engaged in trying to attack his flanks, their center near Pratzen would be stretched very thin. Napoleon intended to strike a powerful blow to smash through this weakened center. Then his troops would be able to defeat the two separated portions of the allied army, one at a time.

Napoleon was in the saddle all day, November 30, riding back and forth to check on the readiness of his units as they occupied their new positions. At the same time he kept a sharp eye on the Russian and Austrian patrols, moving cautiously ahead of their main army through Austerlitz. He set up his own headquarters on Zurlon Hill between the forks of Goldbach Brook, just south of the Olmütz road. From here he could observe the advancing allies and could see that their movements were proceeding as he had expected.

Napoleon had been afraid that the allies might attack him on December 1, which would not give Davout time to arrive. He now knew that Davout, with two small divisions totaling about 8,000 men, would reach Raigern shortly after dark on the night of December 1, and would be available for battle along with the rest of his troops early the next morning. By noon, when he sat down to lunch with his generals, he was confident that the allies would not attack until the following day. He pointed out to the generals that more and more allied troops were shifting to the southwest on the Heights of Pratzen. He was now certain that his plan would work.

5

The Eve
of Battle

Having left his generals on Zurlon Hill, Napoleon checked the disposition of his entire army. He galloped to the extreme left, where a picked regiment of infantry from Marshal Lannes's Fifth Corps was entrenched on a high hill just north of the Olmütz road, supported by a powerful battery of artillery. Under the cover of these guns, Napoleon observed the remainder of Lannes's corps of two divisions, 12,000 strong, drawn up in two powerful lines, completely blocking any allied advance down the main road toward Brünn.

The emperor and his escort then rode about a mile further south. Partially hidden from the allies by hills west of the Gold-bach Brook, Marshal Soult had concentrated two strong divisons of his Fourth Corps—some 17,000 men. Napoleon looked at these troops with satisfaction; they would do well the next day.

Still further to the right, thinly stretched out for three miles in the Goldbach Valley between Kobelnitz and Tellnitz, lay General Legrand's division of Soult's corps, about 8,000 men. Napoleon took time to talk to a number of the officers and men of this division, as they improved their trenches and prepared for battle. This lone division, holding a front more than three miles long, was intended by Napoleon to be the bait which would lure the allies to shift their strength to the south, and thus to weaken their center—where Soult would make the planned main attack. The emperor told Legrand and his men that success depended on their courage and determination.

Napoleon then rode to look at his reserve units. In the left rear, directly behind Marshal Lannes's corps, and massed in deep battalions beside the road, lay Marshal Bernadotte's First Corps, two divisions totaling about 12,000 men. Just south of Bernadotte's troops, three reserve units were concentrated around Napoleon's headquarters hill: Marshal Murat's cavalry corps of about 5,500 men, General Nicolas Oudinot's division of nearly 6,000 men from the Fourth Corps, and 5,000 picked troops of the Imperial Guard under Marshal Jean Bessières.

It was dusk by the time Napoleon had finished this final pre-battle inspection. He returned to his headquarters hut on Zurlon Hill to eat a bite of supper. He prepared a proclamation to be read to the army, then lay down to take a brief nap.

"Long Live the Emperor!"

It was shortly after dark when, by torchlight, the emperor's proclamation was read to the French troops.

> "Soldiers, a Russian army presents itself before you to avenge the Austrian army of Ulm. . . . The positions we occupy are formidable, and while they are marching to turn my right, they will present me their flank.

"Soldiers, I shall myself direct all your battalions. I shall hold myself distant from the fire, if with your accustomed bravery you carry disorder and confusion into the enemy's ranks. But should victory for a moment be uncertain, you will see your Emperor expose himself in the forefront of the battle. For victory must not hesitate, today, especially, where the honor of the French infantry and the honor of all the nation are at stake. . . .

"This victory will finish our campaign; . . . and then the peace I shall make will be worthy of my people, of you and of me."

It was after eight o'clock when Savary awakened Napoleon, as he had ordered before taking his nap. The emperor rose, then strolled down the hill from his headquarters on foot, the collar of his greatcoat raised to protect himself against the cold night air. He wished to listen at the campfires to hear what his soldiers were saying, without being seen. He wanted to know how they

The Eve of
Austerlitz *by*
General Lejeune

had reacted to his proclamation. But he had barely moved up quietly behind one bivouac when he was recognized. Immediately cheers began to rise all around him. Soldiers held high torches of straw and of wood, while cheering "Long live the Emperor! Long live the Emperor!" Some walked in front to light his way with torches and others formed long cheering lines, making bright avenues along which the emperor walked, moved almost to tears by this demonstration of loyalty.

One old soldier marched up to Napoleon, saluted and said, "Sire, you have no need to expose yourself tomorrow. I promise in the name of the grenadiers of the army that you will merely have to fight with your eyes, and that we will carry to you the flags and the artillery of the Russian army to celebrate the anniversary of your coronation."

Such scenes were repeated many times before the elated emperor returned to headquarters on the hill. When he reached the little straw hut which his guards had built, he found Marshal

Davout waiting for him, to report that his two small divisions
were now camped for the night at Raigern. Davout told the
emperor that he had less than 8,000 men with him, and that some
of them had marched ninety miles in the past forty-eight hours.
But he assured Napoleon that they would be able to fight
staunchly the next day, after a night's sleep. Napoleon could see
that Davout, also, was exhausted. Briefly, he explained his plan.
Davout was to be ready to move forward when the enemy attacked the exposed right flank. The trap was complete. Napoleon then patted his marshal on the shoulder and told him to go
back to rest with his troops.

"But you must be on the march by five o'clock," Napoleon
warned.

Davout saluted and left the hut. Napoleon, confident of victory, threw himself down on his field bed and was soon asleep.

Around midnight the emperor was awakened by the sound
of firing from the lower Goldbach Brook, near Sokolnitz. He
jumped from his bed, and sent for Marshal Soult. When Soult
arrived, Napoleon mounted his horse, and galloped with the
marshal to find out what the trouble might be. They learned
that it was only an exchange of musketfire between French and
Russian patrols. The emperor returned to his headquarters and
napped again for about two more hours.

In the Allied Camp

Earlier that evening the allied troops on the Heights of Pratzen
had watched with amazement the sudden flaring of fires and
torches through the French camps. Czar Alexander and Emperor
Francis, accompanied by their senior generals—Kutuzov and
the Austrian Franz von Weyrother—rode out to Pratzen to get
a better look. Since they could not know the real cause, the
allies were puzzled. Finally most of them concluded that the

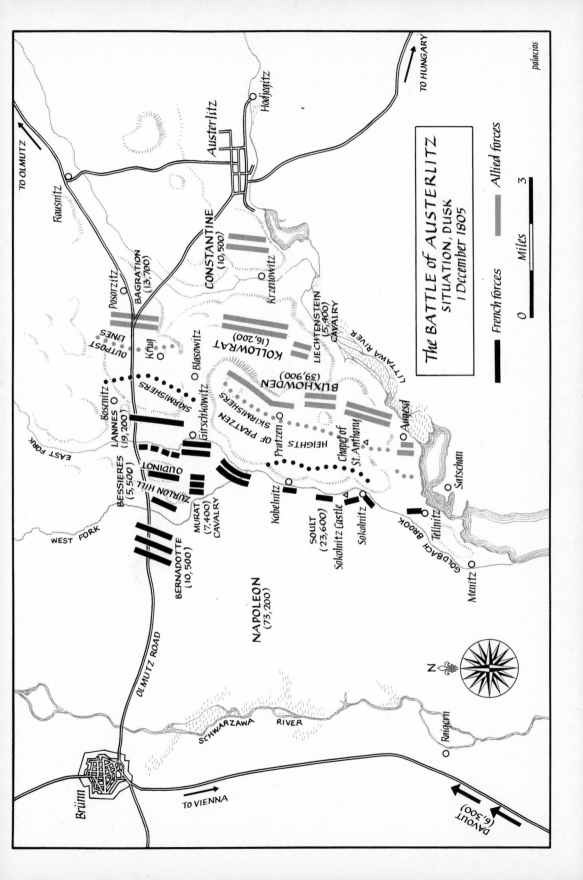

The BATTLE of AUSTERLITZ
SITUATION, DUSK
1 December 1805

French forces
Allied forces

0   Miles   3

palacios

TO OLMUTZ
TO HUNGARY

Hodiegitz
Austerlitz
Rausnitz

Posoritz
BAGRATION
(13,700)

CONSTANTINE
(10,500)

OUTPOST LINES
Krug
Blasowitz
Krzenowitz

Bosenitz
LANNES
(19,200)
SKIRMISHERS
Girschkowitz
KOLLOWRAT
(16,200)
LIECHTENSTEIN
(5,400) CAVALRY

EAST FORK
BESSIERES
(5,500)
ZURLAN HILL
OUDINOT
MURAT
(7,400)
CAVALRY
Pratzen
SKIRMISHERS
BUXHOWDEN
(39,900)
HEIGHTS OF PRATZEN
Chapel of St. Anthony
Augesd
LITTAWA RIVER

WEST FORK
Kobelnitz
SOULT
(23,600)
Sokolnitz Castle
Sokolnitz
Satschan

BERNADOTTE
(10,500)
GOLDBACH BROOK
Tellnitz
Menitz

OLMUTZ ROAD

NAPOLEON
(73,200)

N

Brünn
TO VIENNA

SCHWARZAWA RIVER

Raigern

DAVOUT
(6,300)

General Peter Bagration

French must be making a special display to cover a secret night retreat back along the road to Vienna. Wary old General Kutuzov, however, had had enough experience with Napoleon's wiles to be suspicious of trickery.

The high command now returned to their headquarters at Krzenowitz and entered a tent where the other senior generals were already assembled. Disregarding Kutuzov's objections, Alexander gave the word and Weyrother issued the orders. To prevent the French from escaping, the army must move as soon as possible in the morning. Since this was December, dawn came at 6:30 A.M. The allied corps would begin their movement at 7 A.M. Weyrother explained in detail what each unit was to do. Kutuzov dozed.

As Weyrother explained the plan, the four principal groups of the allied army would combine to form a vast semicircle, a sickle which would hook through and around the right wing of the French army, cutting Napoleon off from his line of communications back to Vienna.

The principal blows would be struck by the left wing and left center—almost two thirds of the allied army—the point and cutting blade of the sickle. Smashing through Napoleon's single, thin right flank division, these allied units would then sweep to the northwest in two parallel left hooks, threatening the line of retreat of the entire French army. At the same time, the allied right wing would advance down the Olmütz road to keep Napoleon's left wing and center busy. In between would be the allied right center; small, fast-moving Austrian and Russian units which would spread out to link the two wings.

The powerful allied left wing, commanded by General Buxhöwden, would attack at dawn across the Goldbach Brook, between Sokolnitz Castle and Tellnitz. This wing consisted of three corps. On the extreme left the 8,500 men of Russian General Doctorov were encamped on the southern slopes of the Pratzen plateau, around St. Anthony's Chapel and the little village of Augesd. Some Austrian cavalry, under General Michael Kienmayer, covered Doctorov's front and left, between Tellnitz and Augesd. Farther north the 12,000 Russians under General Andrault de Langeron—a French émigré—were deployed on both sides of the village of Pratzen. The 14,000 men of Russian General Prszbycewski (pronounced Pribichevski) were bivouacked be-

General Mikhail
Kutuzov

hind Langeron's troops, between Pratzen and the Littawa River.

The allied left center comprised some 25,000 men in two corps under the over-all command of the Austrian General Kollowrat. His own corps and that of the Russian General Miloradovich were encamped for the night on the eastern slopes of the Pratzen plateau. Shortly after dawn they were to follow close behind the northern portion of Buxhöwden's wing, attacking across the Goldbach near Kobelnitz. They were to assist Buxhöwden in smashing through Legrand's weak division, then continue on to cut Napoleon's line of communications to Vienna.

The right center of the allied army, north of Pratzen, consisted only of the Austrian cavalry corps of Prince John of Liechtenstein, about 5,000 strong. But Liechtenstein would be supported in covering the Pratzen plateau by the army's reserve—8,500 crack troops of the Russian Imperial Guard under the Grand Duke Constantine. Weyrother pointed out that Liechtenstein's horsemen, encamped on the central portion of the Pratzen plateau, would have to move out before dawn to reach their assigned positions, since they would have to ride around behind the columns of Kollowrat and Miloradovich.

On the extreme allied right, the Russian corps of General Peter Bagration was bivouacked along the Olmütz road near Rausnitz, north of Austerlitz. These 13,000 men would attack west along the road to Brünn early in the morning, to keep the French left and center from interfering with the flanking movements of Buxhöwden and Kollowrat.

The allied high command was certain of success. They estimated Napoleon's force at about 65,000 men; their own strength was 89,000. Even if they had known that Davout, with his 8,000 reinforcements, was as close at hand as he was, they would have dismissed that addition as negligible. Their great turning movement, coming down from the Heights of Pratzen and moving across the Goldbach Brook, would force Napoleon to retreat. Victory was theirs. Kutuzov alone had any doubts.

6

The Sun of Austerlitz

At 5 A.M. on that fateful day of December 2, 1805, more than an hour before sunrise, Napoleon gulped a hasty breakfast. Like more than 60,000 other French soldiers, he ate a simple but filling meal of soup, bread, and wine. While the emperor and most of the army were eating, however, Davout was already getting his cold and sleepy troops on the march from Raigern.

Soon after six o'clock, as the first streaks of light began to appear in the eastern sky, Napoleon's staff and his other marshals began to assemble on Zurlon Hill. But with the approach of dawn, a heavy mist settled over the countryside. The emperor, already sitting impatiently on his horse, waiting for daybreak, peered through the pre-dawn gloom at the officers around him; there were Berthier, Lannes, Soult, Bernadotte, Bessières, Murat, and Mortier, as well as the faithful Savary and other officers of his personal staff. Then he turned again to the east, hoping to get a glimpse of the sunrise, but was exasperated to find that he could see nothing.

Then, shortly after seven o'clock, the fog slowly began to lift. Suddenly bright sunlight beamed upon the French marshals and generals on the headquarters hill. Those who were with the emperor never forgot this brilliant appearance of the "Sun of Austerlitz," rising like a great ball of golden red over the Heights of Pratzen.

Though the fog lingered in the valley, Napoleon could now clearly see the high ground beyond the brook. The columns of the allied left wing were already on the march, heading south-west into the hazy Goldbach Valley, below the Chapel of St. Anthony, on the southern slopes of the Heights of Pratzen. Joyfully the French emperor called the attention of his generals to the sight. Here was confirmation that the allied plan was proceeding as Napoleon had predicted.

By seven thirty Kienmayer's Austrian cavalrymen were splashing across the Goldbach between Tellnitz and Sokolnitz, drawing fire from the alert French pickets. General Legrand himself

French troops going into battle the morning of December 2nd

was riding up and down behind his thinly extended division, making sure his men were ready for the impending onslaught. He was well satisfied by the cool performance of his entrenched troops, as they repulsed the first Austrian calvalry charge up the western slopes of the narrow valley.

Just then, pouring down from the Heights of Pratzen, barely visible to Legrand through the fog in the valley bottom, came Doctorov's massed battalions. They reached the stream bank, in and around Tellnitz. There the columns hesitated and spread out, each soldier searching for a good wading spot. Covering their advance, Russian cannon began to pound the French positions on the western slopes of the steep valley. Legrand ordered his own artillery to concentrate on the masses of Russian troops crossing the brook.

Goldbach Brook

While the battle raged in and around Tellnitz, the head of Langeron's Russian column was sweeping westward, parallel to Doctorov's. Langeron's men formed a line opposite Sokolnitz, replying with musket and cannon to the intense fire they were receiving from the waiting French troops. Langeron's columns, still pouring down the hillside trails from the Pratzen plateau, were closely followed by Prszbycewski's corps. But Langeron's men were having a hard time crossing the brook under the accurate fire of the outnumbered, but well prepared, French defenders. Since there was no room in the narrow valley for any more troops to deploy, Prszbycewski's battalions were forced to halt on the heights. The corps waited in the bright, thin sunlight, in a long column that stretched back from the edge of the plateau overlooking Sokolnitz as far as the village of Pratzen.

By eight o'clock Napoleon could hear heavy fire all along Goldbach Brook from Sokolnitz Castle to Tellnitz. At the same time he could see the long columns of Russians and Austrians in Kollowrat's and Miloradovich's corps moving over the plateau

A long view
of the Battle
of Austerlitz

past Pratzen, behind the rear of Prszbycewski's column and then down the slopes toward Kobelnitz. By this time the last wisps of fog had disappeared, and the emperor could see down into the valley. He turned to Soult and asked:

"How long will it take you to reach the Heights of Pratzen with your divisions?"

"Less than twenty minutes, Sire," replied the French marshal. Napoleon turned his eyes again toward the heights, and raised his telescope for a long look.

"In that case," Napoleon remarked, "we will wait another quarter of an hour."

By now the Austrians and Russians in the van of the left wing had forced their way across Goldbach Brook. Artillery and musket fire from the French right flank grew more intense. Legrand's division, outnumbered nearly four to one, was forced to give ground. Doctorov drove steadily forward from the crossings at Tellnitz. Langeron captured Sokolnitz while Prszbycewski's leading units were attacking Sokolnitz Castle from three sides.

At this moment, about eight forty-five, fresh troops appeared on Legrand's right. Davout's divisions had arrived. They charged promptly into the left flank of Doctorov's line. The Russians recoiled in the face of this unexpected charge, and many were driven back across the brook. Quickly deploying the rest of his troops, Davout took command of the French right wing. He ordered his own divisions and that of Legrand to counterattack all along the line.

Davout's arrival and the French counterattack momentarily dismayed the Russians. But these were tough soldiers and it did not take them long to recover from their confusion. Doggedly the Russians drove back across the brook. Davout, realizing that he was still heavily outnumbered, pulled his men back to the high ground west of Goldbach Brook. Here, following Napoleon's instructions, he held on with grim determination.

Napoleon surveying the action on the battlefield

Soult's Assault

Shortly before 9 A.M. Napoleon quietly told Soult to start his attack. Galloping down the hill, the French marshal ordered his two division commanders—Generals St. Hilaire and Vandamme —to advance. The two divisions swept across the brook and up to the Heights of Pratzen. Near the crest they smashed into Kollowrat's unsuspecting Russian and Austrian columns, just as their van was approaching Kobelnitz. Some of the startled allied battalions broke and fled.

Kutuzov, accompanying the two monarchs—Alexander and

Francis—had been riding with Kollowrat's columns. Galloping into the thick of the fight, the tough old Russian general formed a hasty defense line near Pratzen. On the extreme left of this line Kutuzov ordered the rearmost units of Prszbycewski's corps to counterattack. These troops had been waiting on the western edge of the plateau, since there had not been room enough for them to deploy into the battle around Sokolnitz Castle. The stout fighting qualities of the Russians briefly halted the French attack. But Soult and his two division commanders at once sent more battalions scrambling up the steep slopes of the plateau in a new assault wave. Slowly but steadily the French pushed the allied center back through Pratzen.

A musket ball struck Kutuzov and he was carried off the field. Czar Alexander sent an aide galloping up to Kutuzov's litter, to inquire if he were badly wounded. "No," replied the old general. Then he waved his hand back toward Pratzen. "There," he said bitterly, "there is the mortal wound."

At the same time that Soult's corps had started its drive across the Goldbach and up toward Pratzen, Bernadotte's two divisions advanced in a great line of massed battalions past Napoleon's headquarters and into the open rolling fields between the corps of Soult and Lannes. Proudly the emperor gazed down from Zurlon Hill at this magnificent display of disciplined troops in their bright uniforms, gay flags flying. As the battalions marched past him he waved his hand in acknowledgement of their deep-throated cheers.

Crossing the brook, Bernadotte's troops began to climb past the village of Girschkowitz and up on to the heights, at first meeting no opposition. Liechtenstein's Austrian cavalry, which was supposed to be guarding the region north of Pratzen, had been delayed south of that village by Kollowrat's advance. But the Grand Duke Constantine's Imperial Guard hastily rushed forward from reserve to meet Bernadotte's advance near Blasowitz. Then, as a terrible struggle began to rage just west of this

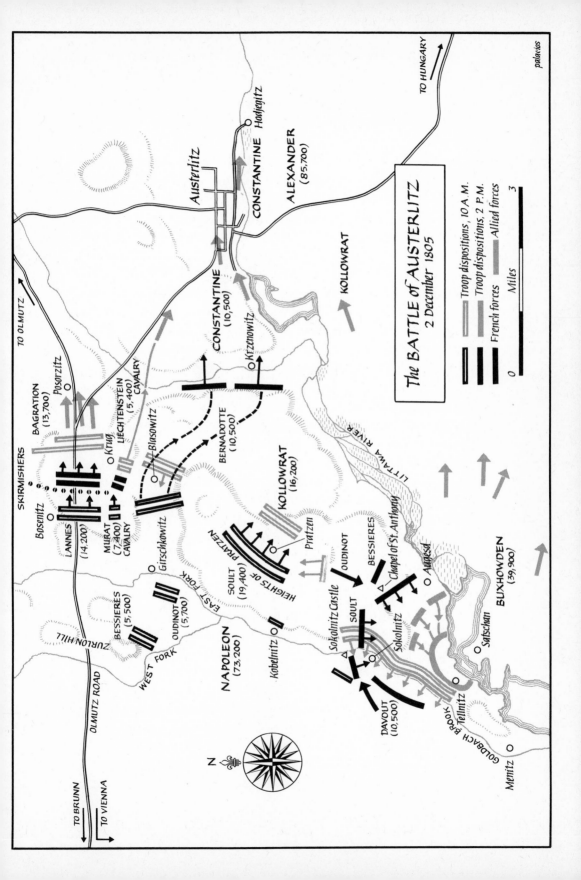

The BATTLE of AUSTERLITZ
2 December 1805

Troop dispositions, 10 A.M.
Troop dispositions, 2 P.M.
French forces
Allied forces

Miles
0   3

TO HUNGARY

palacios

Hodiegitz

CONSTANTINE
ALEXANDER
(85,700)

Austerlitz

KOLLOWRAT

CONSTANTINE
(10,500)

Krzenowitz

TO OLMUTZ

SKIRMISHERS

BAGRATION
(13,700)

Posorzitz

Krug

LIECHTENSTEIN
(5,400)
CAVALRY

Blasowitz

BERNADOTTE
(10,500)

LANNES
(14,200)

Bosenitz

MURAT
(7,400)
CAVALRY

KOLLOWRAT
(16,200)

Girschkowitz

LITTAWA RIVER

HEIGHTS of PRATZEN

Pratzen

Chapel of St. Anthony

BESSIERES

OUDINOT

Augesd

BUXHOWDEN
(39,900)

SOULT
(19,400)

EAST FORK

BESSIERES
(5,500)

OUDINOT
(5,700)

ZURLON HILL

WEST FORK

NAPOLEON
(73,200)

Kobelnitz

Sokolnitz Castle

SOULT

Sokolnitz

Satschan

OLMUTZ ROAD

TO BRUNN

TO VIENNA

DAVOUT
(10,500)

Tellnitz

GOLDBACH BROOK

Menitz

N

village, Liechtenstein's horsemen galloped up on the right of the Russian Guards and began to attack Bernadotte's left flank.

Napoleon, seeing the Austrian cavalry coming into the action, ordered Murat to advance toward Blasowitz to protect Bernadotte's left. The eager French horsemen charged across the brook. In a few moments a tremendous cavalry battle was raging around the villages of Blasowitz and Krug, on the open field between the Olmütz road and the Pratzen plateau.

When Napoleon had sent Soult to attack toward Pratzen, it was as if the French emperor had let fly an arrow aimed directly at a bull's eye—Pratzen—in the center of the allied line. And, with the force of an arrow, Soult was still driving ahead. But Napoleon, observing the action from Zurlon Hill, could now see that this main attack might be in vain if Bernadotte and Murat were unable to hold off the fierce allied counterattacks north of Pratzen. The French emperor galloped forward across the brook to a small hill overlooking Blasowitz, in order to observe this critical part of the fight more closely.

Napoleon, riding up behind General Rivaud's division, on the left of Bernadotte's corps, was immediately recognized by the French soldiers. Word spread through the ranks. Aware that they were fighting under the direct gaze of the emperor, Rivaud's men redoubled the fury of their attacks. By ten o'clock they were in possession of Blasowitz.

The Stubborn Russians

But the Russians were not to be defeated so easily. Constantine's Imperial Guards reformed and counterattacked. Napoleon sent a staff officer, Brigadier General Jean Rapp, to lead a cavalry brigade of his own Guards to the support of Rivaud's hard-pressed division.

The wildest and most intensive fighting of the day now raged briefly around Blasowitz. The finest cavalry regiments of the

Russian Guard, under Prince Repnin, charged recklessly against Rapp's veteran horsemen. Colonel Morland, commanding a regiment of French chasseurs—light cavalry—was killed in the hand-to-hand fighting, and Rapp suffered a sword wound on his head. Ignoring the blood dripping down his face and almost blinding him, Rapp rose in his stirrups and, shouting over the deafening din of the conflict, led one final charge. The Russian line broke. Prince Repnin was captured, and the surviving Russian horsemen fled behind the stubborn line of Constantine's infantry Guards.

By this time Murat's cavalry divisions were also getting the best of Liechtenstein's Austrian cavalrymen, and were threatening Constantine's right. Rivaud's and Drouet's infantry divisions, encouraged by the success of their cavalry comrades, now pressed forward in a shouting bayonet charge. At the same time Rapp led the French cavalry Guards in violent, slashing attacks against the Russian foot soldiers. The pressure was too much even for the best troops in the Russian army; Constantine's men began to give way, falling back toward the Littawa River.

By 11 A.M. the struggle around Blasowitz and Krug was over. Russians and Austrians were retreating in great confusion toward Austerlitz, while Murat and Bernadotte paused briefly to reorganize their forces. Rapp, covered with blood, rode back to report to Napoleon, who had his own doctor care for the wounded general.

Earlier in the morning, shortly after Soult and Bernadotte had led their men up the eastern slopes of the Goldbach Valley, Lannes began to advance directly eastward along the Olmütz road. At the same time General Bagration's Russian corps was moving up from the opposite direction. Shortly before nine-thirty the two forces clashed head-on just southeast of Bosenitz, at the northern edge of the battlefield. They were evenly matched and the fierce struggle raged without advantage to either side for nearly an hour.

By eleven o'clock, however, Bagration could see that the allied troops to his left were being pushed back by Murat and Bernadotte. At the same time his own soldiers were becoming discouraged by the fierceness of the French attacks. Bagration, therefore, began to withdraw slowly eastward along the road, back toward the post house, or inn, of Posorzitz.

The Allied Left Wing

By this time Soult's corps had defeated the allied forces near Pratzen. The remnants of Kollowrat's and Miloradovich's troops were streaming back to Krzenowitz on the Littawa River, while Prszbycewski's right flank was driven back toward Sokolnitz. Under continuing pressure from Bernadotte, the Grand Duke Constantine's Guards were also falling back toward Austerlitz, although they had recovered somewhat from the losses they had suffered around Blasowitz.

It was obvious to Napoleon, shortly after noon, that Soult had pierced the allied center, and that the allied right wing had also been defeated. The first part of the French emperor's plan had been completely successful. The time had come to start the second phase.

Napoleon ordered Soult to halt his pursuit of Kollowrat, and to wheel to his right, behind the allied left wing along Goldbach Brook. The emperor sent orders for Drouet's division of Bernadotte's corps to continue the pursuit of Kollowrat across the Littawa River, while Rivaud and Murat were to follow after Constantine and Liechtenstein toward Krzenowitz and Austerlitz. At the same time Lannes was to keep unceasing pressure against Bagration, who had pulled back behind the Posorzitz post house.

Napoleon and his staff galloped across the Pratzen Heights to join Marshal Soult near the Chapel of St. Anthony, on the south-

LEFT: *Bonaparte confers with one of his staff at Austerlitz.*

ern point of the plateau. Arriving there about 1:30 P.M., the emperor discovered that St. Hilaire's division had already recaptured Sokolnitz Castle, and that Vandamme was preparing to attack to the southwest from St. Anthony's Chapel. The reserve —Bessières's Guards and Oudinot's division—followed behind the emperor to Pratzen, where they were available to move either to the east or to the south. These eager French troops were now fearful they might not see any action. In fact, they never got into the fight.

From the Chapel of St. Anthony Napoleon could look down over Sokolnitz, Tellnitz, and the ponds to the south. He and Soult were now completely behind Buxhöwden's left wing. Few of the soldiers in these three allied corps, intent upon their fierce battle against the stubborn Davout, yet realized their deadly danger.

Davout had been pushed back about a mile west of the Goldbach. While directing the defense of his outnumbered divisions, he had also kept a close watch on the Heights of Pratzen. When he saw Soult's two divisions swing around to attack Buxhöwden's rear, just before 2 P.M., Davout ordered his own troops to counterattack.

Buxhöwden and his men suddenly found themselves assailed by violent French assaults from front and rear. In a few moments the remaining 30,000 soldiers of the allied left wing were thrown into complete disorder. Davout's men were charging toward the brook from the west; Soult's troops advancing southward from the Pratzen plateau.

Only one line of retreat remained for the allies—the open area to the southeast, across the Littawa River swamps, and over the two frozen ponds. Some of the allied soldiers began to surrender at once. A few units, fighting vigorously and determinedly, pulled back across the marshes before Soult could complete the encirclement. The remainder, in great confusion, rushed to cross over the narrow dike between the two ponds; in their haste

The panicked allied retreat over breaking ice

some even ventured to go across the thin ice of the ponds themselves. French artillery now began to fire at these fleeing allied troops. The cannon balls broke the ice; in a few horrible moments hundreds of frantic men and horses were drowned.

Pursuit

The disaster on the ice was the last straw for the panic-stricken troops of the allied left wing. The survivors who had not escaped, or who had not already surrendered, now threw down their arms. In a few minutes one third of the allied army had been destroyed.

Napoleon again mounted his horse and galloped northward to check on the progress of his troops in the center and left. He discovered that Bernadotte's division was pushing across the Littawa River near Krzenowitz, where the Russian Imperial Guard was trying to cover the retreat of the fugitives of the allied center. On the extreme left Lannes had pushed Bagration back past Rausnitz, toward Austerlitz. He had blocked any allied retreat toward Olmütz.

By this time it was about 4 P.M., and already dusk. The short December day was almost over. To prevent his army from drifting apart and dispersing in the darkness, Napoleon ordered his troops to halt in the positions they had then reached. They were to regroup and to be ready to continue the advance the first thing in the morning. Accompanied by his staff, he now made one more tour of the battlefield, covered with terrible piles of dead and wounded scattered over eight miles.

Napoleon learned in the following days that his own army had lost nearly 7,000 men killed and wounded, while allied casualties were about 12,500 with more than 15,000 additional Austrians and Russians taken prisoner. Napoleon's men had also captured 133 allied cannon; nearly fifty more had fallen through the ice in the ponds.

The French troops settled down for the night. Campfires began to blaze brightly in the gathering dark of the winter evening. Napoleon visited each of his corps commanders and most of the division commanders. He wished to satisfy himself that the army was in shape to continue the action on the following day. He also wanted to congratulate his officers and men for their outstanding conduct during the battle.

By midnight the emperor had returned to the Olmütz road, where Lannes's division was bivouacked east of the Posorzitz post house. Here Napoleon decided to establish his headquarters for the night, and to try to catch a few hours' sleep. Going into an upstairs bedroom of the post house, he threw himself, fully

Napoleon touring the field after the battle

clothed, on a bed. In a few moments the exhausted emperor was asleep.

It had been a memorable day. Napoleon had celebrated the anniversary of his coronation by winning one of the most perfectly conceived and executed battles in history.

7

The Peace
of the Emperors

At 4 A.M. on December 3, Napoleon was awakened by the pounding of a fist upon the door of his room. Marshal Berthier, the Chief of Staff, apologized for awakening the emperor at that hour. But the Austrian Prince John of Liechtenstein had just reached the post house under a flag of truce. He had a message from Emperor Francis.

Rising hastily, Napoleon buttoned his collar as he walked downstairs to meet the Austrian emperor's emissary. Saluting, the prince handed him a message. Napoleon glanced at it quickly. Francis asked for an armistice between the two armies, and suggested an early meeting to discuss peace terms.

When Napoleon had gone to bed a few hours earlier, he knew that he had won a tremendous victory. Not till this moment did he realize how badly he had beaten the allies.

But Napoleon was well aware that a request for an armistice could be a trick. Even though badly defeated, the allies might still be able to reorganize and perhaps fight again. Therefore he must push after them promptly so as to give them no rest and no time to regroup. For this reason he told Prince Liechtenstein that he would not grant the armistice. He agreed, however, that he would meet the Austrian emperor the next day, on December 4.

When Liechtenstein asked him where this meeting would take place, Napoleon smiled. He replied that he was sure that the Austrian emperor would have little doubt where he and the French army would be. Liechtenstein understood him well. Napoleon intended to pursue the allies as closely as possible.

On the Heels of the Enemy

Immediately after the Austrian emissary left, Napoleon issued orders for a relentless pursuit. The enemy could have retreated either to the northeast, toward Galicia and Poland, or to the southeast, toward Hungary. Accordingly the emperor ordered his cavalry to scout in both directions.

By noon Napoleon learned from his cavalry scouts that the allies were heading toward Hungary. The two allied emperors had spent the night after the battle in the little village of Hodjegitz, just east of Austerlitz. Through the remainder of the night their generals tried to reorganize their shattered armies. Before dawn the allied retreat had resumed, with Russian and Austrian columns marching as fast as they could toward the Morava River.

Napoleon now shifted his entire army in the same direction. Murat's cavalry continually attacked the Russian and Austrian rear guards, giving them time neither to rest nor to reorganize. By the afternoon of December 4 Napoleon reached Saroschitz, just northwest of Goding (now Hodonin) on the Morava River. Most of the allied army was already across the river at Holitsch (now Holic). In two days they had retreated more than thirty miles, and the French were right at their heels.

The Emperors Confer

An Austrian messenger, under a flag of truce, brought word that
Emperor Francis was coming to meet Napoleon. The French
emperor at once ordered all of his troops to halt their advance.
He and his staff remained at Saroschitz by a ruined mill. Soldiers
of the Imperial Guard built a huge fire beside the mill and
brought a chair so that Napoleon could sit down and keep warm
while waiting. Another chair was brought for the Austrian emperor. The soldiers laid a path of straw from the fire to the road,
so that the two emperors would not have to muddy their boots.

Soon several carriages appeared on the road from Goding,
accompanied by a squadron of Austrian cavalry. As the caval-
cade approached, the French Guards formed in lines on each
side of the road, and presented arms as the leading carriage came
to a halt near the mill. Napoleon walked down the path of straw
as the carriage door opened, and Francis, clad in a handsome
white uniform, stepped out. Greeting the Austrian emperor,
Napoleon offered his hand to assist him in alighting from the
carriage. The two emperors then walked up the straw path toward the fire.

"I regret, Sire," said Napoleon, "that I must receive you here
in the open. But this is the only kind of palace I have had for two
months."

The Austrian emperor was in no mood for joking, but he
smiled wanly as he replied: "You have done so well in getting
yourself to this place, Sire, that I do not think its discomforts
will bother you very much."

It was Napoleon's turn to smile. The two young emperors—
Napoleon was then thirty-six and Francis was thirty-seven years
old—sat down beside the fire to talk peace. They conferred for
nearly an hour. They agreed that the fighting would stop at
once, and that the Russian armies would immediately leave Aus-

tria and return to Russia. Napoleon and Francis also agreed to send their ministers to negotiate a treaty of peace at Pressburg.

Napoleon then escorted Francis back to his carriage. The French guards again presented arms. The two emperors exchanged salutes as the Austrians set out for Goding.

Mounting his own horse, Napoleon said to his staff: "Gentlemen, we return to Paris. The peace is made." He galloped off toward Austerlitz.

Glory Forever

Czar Alexander of Russia, although he refused to make peace with Napoleon, agreed to the truce terms which had been settled between the French and Austrian emperors. Then, while the French army stood aside and let the defeated Russians march past them to the northeast, back to Russia, Alexander sent a message to Napoleon: "Say to your master," Alexander told a French officer, "that I'm going away. He has done miracles. Though your army was smaller than mine, yet it was superior at every point where it attacked."

By these words the Russian emperor showed that he had learned part of the secret of Napoleon's success—but Alexander had not yet learned how Napoleon had accomplished it.

Napoleon issued the following order to his army:

> "Soldiers, I am pleased with you. At Austerlitz you justified all that I expected of your bravery. You have won glory forever for yourselves and your flags. An army of one hundred thousand men, commanded by the emperors of Austria and Russia, has been crushed. . . . From now on you have no rivals to fear. . . . Peace cannot be distant. . . . Soldiers, when we have done all that is necessary to assure the happiness and prosperity of our country, I will lead you back to France. . . . My people will receive you back with joy. . . . When you say, 'I was at the Battle of Austerlitz,' people will reply, 'There stands a brave man.' "

The meeting between emperors Napoleon and Francis

Never again would the sun shine so brightly on Napoleon I, Emperor of the French.

CONSEQUENCES

The Battle of Austerlitz was the first of a series of four great Napoleonic victories that were destined to change the map of Europe and to make the French emperor the dominant figure on the continent. The other three battles—Jena-Auerstadt in 1806, and Eylau and Friedland in 1807—led to the Treaty of Tilsit, where Czar Alexander of Russia and King Frederick William of Prussia were forced to disband the Third Coalition and to acknowledge French supremacy.

But even before this series of brilliant victories culminated at Tilsit, the victory at Austerlitz had had historic consequences. By the terms of the Peace of Pressburg, signed on December 26, 1805, Austria was forced to give up her possessions in Italy to French control; she also had to cede the Tyrol and Vorarlburg to Bavaria and several smaller districts to Würtemberg and Baden. With this territory, Austria also lost about three million subjects.

It was now obvious to Emperor Francis that the Holy Roman Empire—for almost a thousand years the traditional empire of Germany—had become meaningless. It was, as Voltaire had written a few years earlier, "neither holy, nor Roman, nor an empire." Furthermore, as a result of the French victories at Ulm and Austerlitz, Napoleon controlled more of the empire's territory than Francis. So, on August 6, 1806, Holy Roman Emperor Francis II announced the end of the old empire; henceforth he was to be known as Francis I, Emperor of Austria.

Of even deeper and more far-reaching significance were the political and social changes that were brought about by Napoleon's victories and the Peace of Tilsit—changes that began immediately after the Battle of Austerlitz. Although hereditary monarchs were to rule nations from their inherited thrones for

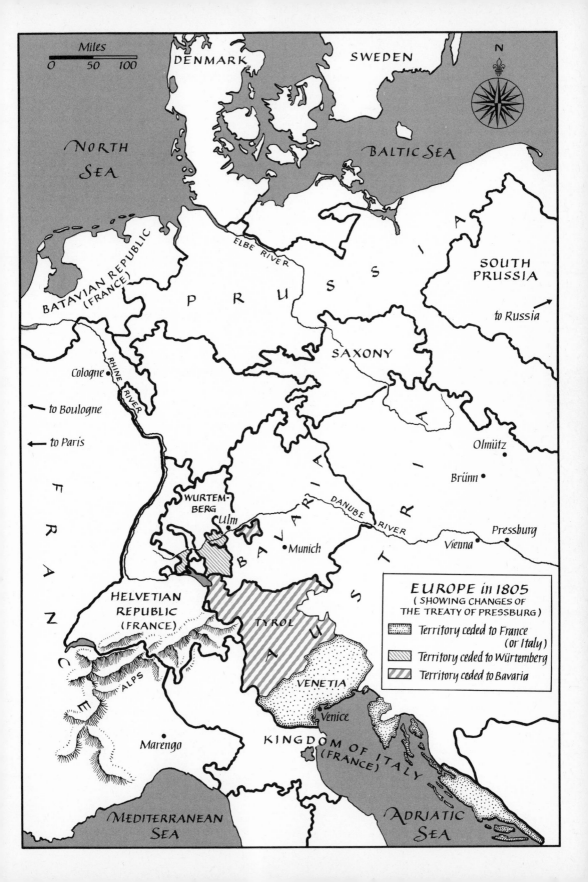

generations to come, the monarchial system began to change. No longer were privileges doled out to a favored few who claimed noble birth while the great mass of the people lived in deprivation. No longer could national boundaries serve as a bar to the changes already brought about in France by the French Revolution. The new ideas—the rise of a middle class, the concept of equal rights and justice for all, backed up by a codified system of government and law—washed over Europe in an invisible tide, never permanently to retreat.

Not the least of the consequences of Austerlitz was its effect on Napoleon's own career. He could rightly look upon it as the perfect battle, a masterpiece of foresight, intuition, and care for detail, one which he executed as brilliantly as he had planned it. Napoleon was too intelligent ever to believe that the exact circumstances of that battle could be re-created. And many times in later years he was to demonstrate the same matchless skill which had won that battle. But the ease with which he had won the battle and the results it achieved for him led the emperor to half-believe the fawning courtiers who told him he was invincible. Even to the end of his career he felt that, if need be, he could always create another Austerlitz.

Furthermore, the great victory whetted his already great ambition and caused him to have less concern for the rights and privileges of other people. As a young officer fighting for the Revolution, Napoleon had opposed the tyranny of the French kings. But now he began to use methods just as ruthless, and just as tyrannical, to further his ambition to become the most powerful man in the world. He became more interested in using the ideals of the French Revolution to make enemy rulers unpopular than he was in trying to improve the living conditions of the common people. And though his efficient government had made France prosperous, his wars were destined to undo much of his good work, and to bring sorrow, misery, and hardship to most of the French people. They would bring Napoleon himself to defeat and ruin in Russia and at Waterloo.

Chronology

JULY 14, 1789.   The Bastille falls; the French Revolution begins.

AUGUST–DECEMBER, 1793.   Siege of Toulon.

OCTOBER 5, 1795.   General Bonaparte puts down a royalist uprising in Paris which threatens to overthrow the republican government.

1796–1797.   First Italian Campaign.

1798–1799.   Egyptian Expedition.

NOVEMBER 9, 1799.   Napoleon seizes power in a *coup d'état*.

DECEMBER 24.   Napoleon is appointed First Consul.

JUNE 14, 1800.   Napoleon defeats a large Austrian army in Italy at the Battle of Marengo.

MARCH 27, 1802.   England, discouraged by the failure of her efforts to overthrow the French Republic, makes peace in the Treaty of Amiens.

MAY 16, 1803.   England again declares war on France.

JUNE 14.   Napoleon establishes his *Grande Armée* at Boulogne.

MAY 18, 1804.   Napoleon declares himself Emperor of France.

DECEMBER 2.   At his coronation, Napoleon crowns himself Emperor and Josephine Empress.

JANUARY–AUGUST, 1805.   Through secret negotiations Austria, Russia, and England, joined by Sweden and Naples, establish the Third Coalition and begin to plan a joint invasion of France.

AUGUST 3.   Napoleon arrives at Boulogne to prepare for a strike at England across the Channel.

AUGUST 26.   Learning through his spies that Austria and Russia plan to attack his rear while he is focusing on the English Channel, Napoleon orders his army to march from Boulogne to Vienna. He plans to strike the unsuspecting allies while they are still completing their mobilization.

AUGUST 28.   Napoleon's army, totaling about 195,000 men, starts its march east.

SEPTEMBER 2.   An Austrian army, about 120,000 men under General Karl Mack von Lieberich, begins its advance toward the Rhine. Near Ulm Mack plans to meet with two Russian armies under General Mikhail Kutuzov and General Friedrich von Buxhöwden and cross the Rhine into France.

SEPTEMBER 26.   Napoleon's army crosses the Rhine and enters Germany.

OCTOBER 7.   The French army begins to cross the Danube between Donauwörth and Ingolstadt.

OCTOBER 17–20.   General Mack, his line of retreat to Austria cut off by Napoleon, surrenders at Ulm.

OCTOBER 20.   The French army marches toward Vienna.

OCTOBER 21.   The French fleet is defeated by Admiral Horatio Nelson at Trafalgar.

NOVEMBER 11.   Battle of Durrenstein. General Kutuzov defeats a small section of the French army under Marshal Edouard Mortier.

NOVEMBER 13.   Vienna falls to Napoleon.

NOVEMBER 15.   Napoleon's army drives back the Russian rear guard at Hollabrunn.

NOVEMBER 19–20.   Kutuzov's retreating Russians and Austrians join Buxhöwden's army near Olmütz in Bohemia. The Russian Emperor Alexander takes command of the combined allied army. Its total strength is 89,000 men.

NOVEMBER 21.   Napoleon moves his headquarters to Brünn.

NOVEMBER 27.   The allied army begins to march south from Olmütz.

NOVEMBER 28.   Napoleon assembles about 65,000 men between Brünn and Austerlitz.

NOVEMBER 29–30.   Napoleon withdraws his outposts from Austerlitz and Pratzen, pulls his army behind the Goldbach Brook, concentrating most of his forces near the Brünn-Olmütz road.

DECEMBER 1.   The allies concentrate their troops between Austerlitz and Pratzen. Marshal Louis N. Davout's two divisions reach Raigern.

DECEMBER 2, 5:00 A.M.   The French army forms up for battle; Davout marches east from Raigern.

7:00 A.M.   The allied left wing, commanded by General Buxhöwden, marches to envelop the French right.

7:00–7:15 A.M.   "The Sun of Austerlitz" appears over the Heights of Pratzen.

7:30–8:00 A.M.   General Kienmayer's Austrian cavalrymen draw fire from French pickets between Tellnitz and Sokolnitz.

8:30 A.M.   The Russians and Austrians in the van of the allied left wing seize crossings of the Goldbach.

8:45 A.M.   Napoleon orders Marshal Nicholas Soult to advance on Pratzen. Davout's fresh troops arrive at the Goldbach. Davout takes command of the French right wing; his divisions, along with those of General Legrand, counterattack between Tellnitz and Sokolnitz.

9:00 A.M.   Soult strikes General Kollowrat's Russian and Austrian troops at Pratzen.

—— General Jean Baptiste Bernadotte's two divisions advance on Soult's left.

—— Marshal Jean Lannes's troops begin to advance eastward along the Olmütz road.

—— Murat's cavalry advances toward Blasowitz to protect Bernadotte's left.

9:00–11:00 A.M.   Soult drives Kollowrat from the Heights of Pratzen. Bernadotte seizes and holds Blasowitz against General Constantine's Russian Imperial Guards.

9:00 A.M.–1:00 P.M.   Engagement along the Goldbach. In stubborn fighting, Davout is driven back about one mile.

9:30–10:30 A.M.   Murat and Liechtenstein's cavalrymen are engaged between Krug and Blasowitz.

9:30 A.M.–12:00 noon.   Lannes' troops clash with General Bagration's Russian Corps between Bosenitz and Posorzitz.

11:00 A.M.–1:00 P.M.   Soult wheels south to the Chapel of St. Anthony and Sokolnitz to attack Buxhöwden's rear; Bernadotte's division pursues Kollowrat across the Littawa River; Murat and Rivaud drive Constantine and Liechtenstein back across the Littawa near Krzenowitz.

12:00 noon–5:00 P.M.   Lannes pushes Bagration back past Rausnitz toward Austerlitz.

1:00–2:00 P.M.   Soult's two divisions, advancing south from the Pratzen Plateau, attack Buxhöwden's rear; Davout strikes the allied left wing toward the Goldbach from the west.

2:00–4:00 P.M.   Collapse and dispersal of allied left wing.

2:00 P.M.–6:00 P.M.   Allied center and right retreats through Austerlitz to Hodjegitz.

12:00 midnight.   Napoleon establishes headquarters at the Posorzitz Post House.

DECEMBER 3, 4:00 A.M.   Prince John of Liechtenstein delivers Austrian Emperor Francis II's request to Napoleon for an armistice and conference to discuss peace terms.

DECEMBER 3–4.   The French pursue the allies to the Morava River. On December 4, Napoleon confers with Francis. They agree that hostilities will end and that the Russian armies will immediately leave Austria and return to Russia.

DECEMBER 26.   The Treaty of Pressburg is signed. By its terms, Austria cedes her possessions in Italy to the French, Tyrol and Vorarlburg to Bavaria, and several small districts to Würtemberg and Baden.

For Further Reading

BARRÈS, JEAN-BAPTISTE. *Memoirs of a Napoleonic Officer*, translated by Bernard Miall. New York: The Dial Press, Inc., 1925.

BELLOC, HILAIRE. *Napoleon*. Philadelphia: J. B. Lippincott Co., 1932.

CHANDLER, DAVID. *The Campaigns of Napoleon*. New York: The Macmillan Co., 1966.

DODGE, THEODORE AYRAULT. *Napoleon*. Boston: Houghton Mifflin Co., 1904.

GUERARD, ALBERT. *Napoleon I*. London: Hutchinson & Co. Ltd., 1957.

LUDWIG, EMIL. *Napoleon*. New York: The Modern Library, Inc., edition undated.

SAVANT, JEAN. *Napoleon in His Time*, translated by Katherine John. New York: Thomas Nelson & Sons, 1954.

WARTENBURG, YORCK VON. *Napoleon as a General*. West Point: U.S.M.A. Press, edition undated.

Index